THE EVE O

THE EVE OF
Persecution

BASILEA SCHLINK

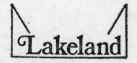

LAKELAND
116 Baker Street
London W1M 2BB

Manuscript completed by July 15, 1973

First British Edition – 1974

ISBN 0 551 00525 4

Printed in Great Britain by
Hunt Barnard Printing Ltd., Aylesbury, Bucks.

TABLE OF CONTENTS

FACING THE
FACTS

A Well-organized Plan

Top-secret Communist training information with instructions for agents, which was carefully guarded only a few years ago, is now accessible to the public. One book on this topic, for instance, states the most important tactics for the political and intellectual conquest of a nation, saying, 'By psychopolitics* our chief goals are effectively carried forward. To produce a maximum of chaos in the culture of the enemy is our first most important step. Our fruits are grown in chaos, distrust, economic depression and scientific turmoil.'[1] With these aims in mind, trained secret agents sow their ideas in all government institutions, universities, schools, hospitals, military colleges, as well as Christian organizations, and above all, in mental health groups. To this end every existing form of Christian ministry must be swept aside; the foundations of the Christian faith undermined. Agents are commissioned to turn every professor, teacher, doctor, psychiatrist, politician into a tool of the Communist psychopolitical doctrine – with or without their knowledge. Agents must labour until they have control over the minds and bodies of every important personage in the land.

* 'Psychopolitics is the art and science of asserting and maintaining dominion over the thoughts and loyalties of individuals, officers, bureaux, and masses, and the effecting of the conquest of enemy nations through "mental healing".'[2]

3

Everyone under control? – But how? Modern training courses, conferences and lectures are being held, adapted to the milieu – whether it be an economic council, church conference, religious retreat, Christian youth group, teacher training college, the army or even a primary school class. In all areas of society Sensitivity Training* has found its niche.[3] Everyone is being introduced to it and in each case this corrosive psychopolitical drug is packaged and labelled differently. 'Developing mutual understanding in society'; 'Improving interhuman relationships'; 'Creating equality between nations, races, classes and in families'; 'How to win respect'; 'How to become well-adjusted and more sensitive to others'; 'How to turn your group or fellowship into a well-functioning organism'.

Most people are ignorant of the true aims of Sensitivity Training. It appears to be a party game. It is new and interesting. It seems to provide an acceptable way, at last, for the ego to receive sympathy and understanding. The initiators, however, know better and are out for more. For many of the trained group leaders, Sensitivity Training is part of the change-over programme in a world-wide, atheistic scheme, known as psychopolitics. These leaders manipulate the opinions of the individuals and of the group in such a way that most of them do

---

* Cover names for Sensitivity Training: T-Group Training, Group Dynamics, Auto-Criticism, Operant Conditioning, Human Relations, Synanon Games Clubs, Basic Encounter Group, Broad Sensitivity, Class in Group Counselling, Management Development, Leadership Class, Self-Honesty Session, Self-Examination, Interpersonal Competence, Interpersonal Relations, Self-Evaluation, Human Potential Workshop, Transactional Analysis (T.A.) . . .

not realize it. Although a feeling of guilt is awakened in the participants (which will make a Christian, for example, admit that he has failed to live as he should), the person is told that he is not at fault, but rather his environment – his parents brought him up wrong; the structure of society did not let him develop his personality; the Church and her teachings made him inhibited, etc. Consequently, feelings of aggression are elicited. Having been 'liberated' from their former moral standards and other codes of life, the participants are all made uniform and arrive at a common understanding. Such brainwashing is effective. No longer inhibited and bound by loyalty to their family, church or faith, and deadened to their consciences, people begin to be useful tools of Communism by carrying out the ideas with which they have been indoctrinated. The manipulation is in progress. Today people are being turned into revolutionaries; tomorrow they will become impersonalized 'world citizens' ideal for a world-wide Communist state under strict dictatorship.

Later, in order to set up this world government, those in key positions who are opposed to Sensitivity Training will be brought under suspicion of insanity. In mental institutions a person can be made incurably mentally ill, through shock treatment or brain surgery. Consequently, he is deprived of all rights and his resistance is broken down.[4]

'Religion must be made synonymous with neurosis and psychosis.'[5] The psychopoliticians are working for the day when the public will be convinced that the Christian standards for good and evil are the main causes of mental illness. Plans were made for dedicated Communists to infiltrate all health institutions posing as qualified advisers in order to ensure that these institutions join in the campaign against religion. 'While we today seem to be kind to the Christian remember we have yet to influence the "Christian world" to our ends. When that is done, we shall have an end of them everywhere.'[6]

In 1945-6 in Warsaw a very extensive Communist plan for infiltration was conceived.[7] The main tactics were to avoid any direct action against religious groups in future; to stop persecuting Catholics and Protestants; but to use the indirect method instead, by forming an alliance with the enemy of Marxism, weakening it and destroying it from within. Students with strong Communist convictions should enrol in seminaries to become priests and win the confidence of the superiors through excellent scholarship, diligence and assumed devotion. After their ordination they should strive for key positions and begin the work of destruction.

A 'Secret Document for the Party's Activities Abroad' from Office No. 106 of China's Communist Party, dated February 12, 1957, reads: 'Catholicism and Protestantism are two organizations that work for capitalistic imperialism. Our comrades must make every attempt to penetrate their heart, since these two churches that are established throughout the world are spreading the poison of their teachings against socialism everywhere. All leading comrades should remember that the Church is an instrument of imperialism and for that reason it must be completely annihilated.' In the nine items of the 'Secret Document' specific instructions were given. Agents should obtain places in church schools to mix with students; deliberately take part in all church activities. They should be baptized in order to become members of the Church; join Christian organizations under false pretexts; use high-sounding words so as to win Christians for themselves; refer continually to the love of God and defend the cause of peace in order to create a radical division between the different groups of believers later. They should make contact with the clergy and spy on their activities. But they should carry out all these instructions maintaining an air of extreme friendliness, according to the precept, 'Conform to the enemy in order to crush him.'[8]

Another method is being applied to obtain world dominion; it is conceived by the hatred of God, which is the source of Communism. Whoever hates God hates His commandments; so from the very outset the dissolution of God's commandments has been part of the battle. Communism intends to dispose of the 'old-fashioned, petty bourgeois morality', the Christian standards of good and evil.

The 'Secret Document' of February 12, 1957 also states that the comrades should enter the heart of church activities, and in order to make headway they should take advantage of the seductive powers of the female sex. Similar instructions can be found elsewhere, declaring that through sex a person can be made to do anything. Sensitivity Training and sex are the two blades of the pair of scissors being used by one and the same hidden hand.

The Communist Party of Italy informed its members in the film industry of its policy to advocate pornography, condone homosexuality and promote films of this nature. 'We . . . praise actors in such plays as champions of freedom . . . They are in effect ants working voluntarily and without pay for us as they eat away the very roots of bourgeois society.'[9] The Italian and French film industry, controlled by labour unions that are highly Communistic, are deliberately producing pornographic films and foisting them upon other countries.[10]

The move towards the breakdown of morals has also become obvious in the Communist infiltration of the Church during the past decades. Nowadays even within the realm of the Church sexual perversions are approved of.[11] In a pamphlet issued by the National Council of Churches in the United States, entitled, *Called To Responsible Freedom, The Meaning Of Sex In The Christian Life*, that was designed for young people looking for a guide to the relationship between the sexes, it states, 'For the Christian there are no laws, no rules, no regulations . . .'[12] Referring to the Commandment against adultery, for example, it concludes that Jesus was 'seeking to set men free from this sort of legalistic bondage.'[13]

No Need for Camouflage

The day of secret handbooks, counterfeit goals, and secret instructions is almost past. As early as 1970 in Britain posters were distributed with the challenge: 'Prepare for Revolution!' 'It is our intention to take power away from these persons in authority and to put it directly into the hands of the British worker . . . We shall do this by organizing and enlisting support for a General Strike . . . we shall defeat the Government and take control of all administration. We are an organized, revolutionary and representative committee . . . We have the militant qualifications and the funds necessary to carry out our task . . . Our country is in the hands of the capitalist swine including Labour Party millionaires . . . We have only ourselves to blame for having been slow to change the structure of our society. But it is not too late for us to take power into our hands . . . Prepare for Revolution! . . . You can help to create chaos in your place of work. You can do your part by defying authority in every way . . . Pass this copy round. Let everyone read it in your place of work.'[14]

Shortly afterwards a new poster appeared: 'We need to have a change of system and to do that, we need a Revolution . . . This time, it will be the biggest TAKE-OVER BID we have ever seen. It will be a TAKE-OVER BID by the working people and there will be no prison in the land large enough to accommodate all the millions of honest working people on General Strike everywhere against the capitalist Labour Government . . . Prepare for Revolution! Prepare to occupy your factory!'[15]

In November 1971 in West Germany leaflets with printed membership cards were distributed by the 'Anti-imperialism League' in many households. The leaflets read as follows: '. . . The time when a handful of imperialistic robbers could pose as masters of the world is finally over. In the vast territories of Asia, Africa and Latin America, where two thirds of the world's population live, militant revolutionary movements among the people are gathering force. They are growing increasingly violent, gaining one victory after another, and drowning the imperialists and their lackeys in the sea of civil war. Today the heroic battle of the peoples of Indochina is a glowing example of nations fighting for national freedom and independence. Their battle has demonstrated . . . that a people, when it has the courage to begin an armed, revolutionary battle and to take the destiny of its country into its own hand, can win the final victory over an imperialistic world power . . .' This 'Anti-imperialism League' promises to institute work groups and training sessions. It intends to devote all its energy to make headway in all classes of society and create a broad unified anti-imperialistic front. Indeed, wherever we look, plans that were once held secret are now being openly propagated.

What Dimitri Manuilsky, leader of the Comintern, predicted years ago is being fulfilled before our very eyes. In 1931 he declared, 'Today we are not strong enough to attack. Our time will come in thirty or forty years. In order to win we need an element of surprise. The bourgeoisie must be put into a coma. One day we will begin to set up the most theatrical peace movement that has ever existed. The capitalistic countries, stupid and decadent, will work with pleasure towards their own destruction. They will be completely deceived by a new opportunity for friendship with us and as soon as they are off their guard, we will crush them with clenched fists.'[16]

Capitalistic countries are working towards their own destruction? This happens, for example, when governments pass legislation allowing certain tendencies to gain a foothold in the educational system. In West Germany more and more nursery schools are to be government-run and the Christian ones will have to close down. As a result children will be removed from all Christian influence. On the other hand, the door is being opened wide for the infiltration of the anti-authoritarian and Communist thought patterns that are pervading education today.

A letter from France: 'A great number of our teachers are Communists, Trotskyites and Maoists. The private schools, which are mainly church-affiliated, are to be taken over by the state. Our epoch reminds us of the one directly preceding the French Revolution.'

In Hesse, a county in West Germany, a battle is being waged for the radical reform of the school system. A socialist teachers' union in Frankfurt recommends socialist literature for children. *Five Fingers Make a Fist* is the title of a book for children three years of age and older, whereas children over nine are given a provocative story against landlords.

Extreme leftist terror groups – for example 'red cells', 'black cells', and 'anti-authoritarian militant groups' – are springing up like mushrooms. They thrive especially well in the university climate. A leaflet circulated at an SDS* meeting in America reveals the typical guiding principles of such organizations. 'Until the student is willing to destroy TOTALLY and JOYFULLY those repressive structures – to attack and destroy the bourgeois social order – his student movement will always be just that – never truly revolutionary . . . The buildings are yours for the burning, for until they are destroyed, along with civilization . . . YOU will not live.'

And words are translated into action. In America, for instance, a young extreme leftist involved in the bombing of a campus ROTC† building said that he felt a moral obligation deep down inside of him to destroy what he hated. Otherwise, he would have felt guilty.[17]

Communists are setting up front organizations with the aim of seizing power during large-scale riots. In city districts and industries, cells are being formed and newspapers for young people are published. Today there is open talk of the 'day of take-over' and all opponents – not just the political ones – are threatened with violence and retaliation after the take-over.

Other Communist groups, for the time being, have assumed a gentler tone for tactical reasons. To the public they appear to be 'quite respectable organizations', according to the press – until an opportune moment arises when it pays to use terror and violence. Then they will launch into action as a sharp weapon of world Communism. We are being threatened on

* SDS – Students for a Democratic Society.
† ROTC – Reserve Officers' Training Corps.

both sides – by Maoist and Soviet Communism.

Delegations of the Communist parties of France and Italy met in Rome in May 1973 to plan Communist undertakings, to seek common enterprises for Communists and Socialists as well as representatives from Catholicism.

In the past ten years Communism has made such headway that it has subverted the Christian nations. Young people in particular live in the philosophy of Marx and Mao and put it into practice, as the student revolts during the past five years prove. Mr Horchem of Hamburg, President of the Committee for the Protection of the West German Constitution, ascertained in August 1973 that 'the Marxists have already succeeded in keeping most of the West German universities in a constant state of turmoil. Although only fifteen per cent of the 670,000 students are politically active, most of the activists are Marxists . . . They control almost all of the student councils at the sixty-seven universities and technical colleges in the country . . .'[18] Even in many of the German high schools there are extreme leftist groups in the student body. The objectives of Communism have been attained to a great extent. As early as 1962 the Venezuelan bishops wrote in a pastoral letter for their country, 'With extraordinary dexterity and doggedness Communism has penetrated all areas of national life, placing its adherents in key positions.' [19]

Indeed, Communism has not only introduced its ideas in government institutions and organizations – universities, schools, labour unions, hospitals, etc. – but it has many church institutions under control through Communist agents, or persons who are commissioned to work for them or who are unwitting tools of Communist ideology. Arrangements are being made for the day of take-over, and this day will come soon.

Don't Be Deceived!

Do we realize what a take-over by Communism involves? It means that we are standing on the verge of Christian persecution, for war against imperialism is war against the Church, which Communists regard as 'an instrument of imperialism'. And this war, Marx proclaimed long ago, justifies the use of violence. What used to be pure theory is increasingly being put into practice. Bloodshed and acts of violence are growing more and more frequent. A group of young Christians involved in outreach and evangelism in Scandinavia was followed by a Communist who told them openly, 'You Christians, ... We have planned your end!'

Persecution of Christians is about to break out throughout the world and it will come soon – before the world disaster is touched off by a nuclear war. What Christian persecution entails nowadays is apparent from reports from the USSR and other lands behind the Iron and Bamboo Curtains where millions have been liquidated. War against Christians, since it is ultimately war against God, is an integral part of Communism, whose main tenet is the equalization of all men and the overthrow of all authority. But the Supreme Authority, who in turn institutes every true authority on earth, is God. Communism lives and works zealously for the deposing of this divine Authority, thus concentrating its

17

hatred on the Lord of lords, God and His Son, Jesus Christ, for as Marx wrote in the preface of his dissertation, 'The Creed of Prometheus': "In a word, I utterly hate each and every God!"[20] It necessarily follows that one of the maxims of Communism is that every Communist must be an atheist; each one is obligated to work for the 'abolition of religion'. Not only the Christians will come under this attack, but also the Jews, for this hatred is directed at all who believe in the living God.

Yet a haze of deception and lies seems to have spread over mankind, including the Christian world. People dream of peaceful co-existence and co-operation with the Communists, deluded by their apparent sincerity. Many naively believe them when they declare their programme for unity and world peace, a golden future, true brotherhood, the uniform distribution of goods, liberty, equality, justice – a utopian state . . . Many believe these Party slogans, although the dreadful truth about these attractive offers is known. Authors opposed to the regime disappear into mental institutions; millions are suffering in concentration camps. Over 120 million people have been killed – 44.5 million in Russia, 34.2 million in Red China (not including the 40 million said to have been liquidated during the Chinese Cultural Revolution), and 3.2 million in Eastern Europe.[21]

What do the Communist slogans mean in practice? Instead of freedom – suppression of opinion and deadening of conscience. Instead of equality – dictatorship, a ruling class, possessing all the power and resources. Instead of justice – cruel despotism and even torture. Instead of paradise – hell on earth.

18

Thus the methods for bringing 'emancipated man' and a 'new society' into existence can only have the same origin. If a person does not conform to the system and agree with its objectives, he can be made to comply by the PDH method (pain, drugs, hypnosis). Undernourishment, privation of sleep, torture and drugs weaken resistance before hypnosis is applied.[22] Thus, concentration camps, prisons, torture and the most ingenious methods of hypnosis are all part of the scheme.

Such horror awaits us when Communism takes over – especially, if we are Christians. There is enough information about Christian persecution in Russia, in other countries behind the Iron Curtain and in Red China to give us a vivid picture of what the future holds for us. In order to evade the issue of such future suffering, many of the Christians who have not changed their loyalties merely close their eyes. The truth is suppressed; deception is preferred; the need for preparation is ignored.

The real danger, however, is not the political concept of Communism. There are other powers at work that are behind atheism, instigating hatred against God and Christianity. Communism and capitalism form an antithesis, but they have a common denominator, for the roots of atheism are present in both. These two main ideologies stem from godless materialism, which aims at a life detached from God and in opposition to His authority. While Communism uses mass terror to force people to comply, capitalism, in its quest for power, seeks the highest profit and greatest progress in science and economics. Behind it all is the great adversary of God, a fact

19

which mankind in its blindness fails to see.

But God intends to open blind eyes. He does not want us to be deceived by promises of a golden future of freedom and justice – promises which will bring us destruction and terror, hell on earth and in eternity instead. To open our eyes, He lets Satan emerge from his concealment today and show his true face.

Satanism – Religion or Politics?

On May 1, 1776 Adam Weishaupt, a Professor of Canon Law, founded the 'Order of the Illuminati' in Ingolstadt, Bavaria. Five years before that he was initiated into alchemy and witchcraft, and under the cover of the Freemason Lodge in Munich he carried out occult practices. However, the Order of the Illuminati that was established as an atheistic institution not only practised occultism and Satanism, but also pursued political goals:

(1) the overthrow of government and abolition of all religions, especially Christianity;
(2) the instigation of chaos by revolutions and wars in order to seize power and set up a totalitarian world government with Satanism as the compulsory state religion.

Was Weishaupt a megalomaniac who came to a miserable end, leaving no adherents behind – a man of no significance? Indeed not. He was a stone in Satan's hand to start an avalanche rolling – an avalanche of widespread death and horror.

The members of his order were, for instance, Voltaire, Mirabeau and Robespierre. In France the most fanatical group of Freemasons, the Jacobins, joined the Illuminati. They were the instigators of the gruesome French Revolution, which ended in the blood bath of Christians. Weishaupt, later called 'the patriarch of the Jacobins', was known as 'Spartakus' in his own order. Later this name was to reappear in Germany after the First World War as the name of a Marxist group, the 'Spartakists', who caused violent riots in 1918-19. One member involved was the philosopher Herbert Marcuse, who still wields great influence. In 1919 the Communist Party of Germany grew out of the Spartakus League, and today there is a Marxist student movement afoot in West Germany that calls itself 'Spartakus'. The most important ideologies that developed from the philosophy of the Illuminati, their Satanism and their hatred of God and the Christians, are Communism, anarchism, National Socialism and Fascism.[23]

Today a sudden jet of water is spurting from the underworld, spewing its fiendish poison high into the air. The connection of this new diabolical trend with the past is unmistakable. A high priest of Satan called the 'Black Pope', Anton LaVey, who started a Satanist movement, substantiates his theses by referring to those of Weishaupt, whom he calls a 'practising Satanist'. LaVey drives a car with the licence plate 'SATAN 9', has a black house in San Francisco with a 'ritual chamber' for Satan. He has written *The Satanic Bible*, a mixture of magic, socialism and sex. At Satanic weddings and other rituals the altar is a naked woman. In the initiation ceremony the prospective member must sign himself over to the devil with his own blood. Sacrilegious and blasphemous services known as 'black masses' are held; records are then made of them and put into circulation. On such records the sound of a crucifix

22

being broken and people swearing allegiance to 'our lord Satan' can be heard.

Just like the preliminary stages initiated by Weishaupt the Satanic cult is not merely an insignificant oddity. Satan's influence today is spreading like wildfire throughout the world. LaVey himself said that the Satanic Age started in 1966 when God was declared dead, when the Sexual Freedom League came into prominence and the hippies formed their free sex culture. [24]

From that point on Satanic cults have expanded in every major city of the United States. At the beginning of 1971 in a small town in America 450 Satanist priests were ordained. At Easter in the same year 4,000 people gathered in Chicago to worship Satan. 'In Michigan, one book store near a college is selling 100 copies of the Satanic Bible for every one copy of the Bible.' [25]

There are Satan worshippers in other countries apart from the United States; in West Germany, Great Britain, Switzerland, France – indeed, throughout the world. Even years ago in England parts of black masses were shown on television. The pictures on the screen changed with lightning speed, alternating in rapid succession from familiar Christian ceremonies to nude scenes and Satanic orgies performed round an altar.

On May 12, 1973 a West German television station televised a documentary film on 'Religion from the Underground', which included portions of a black mass. The consecrated wafers were passed round to the words, 'Become part of the devil's body.' During 'cultic rituals' incense was mixed with hashish;

23

whisky and other alcoholic drinks were handed round. The most infernal music provided the background for these vile scenes.

For centuries now Satan's policy has been to spread the belief that he does not exist. Today as he comes out of hiding, he betrays his existence in his passionate hatred of God, of Christians and their churches and meetings. In 1966 he used Anton LaVey to found the Church of Satan as a counter-church. Previously such occult groups had to meet under the cover of secret societies; whereas now the Church of Satan is registered as a religious body in America. In the past Satan kept his devious plans well hidden, in the underground, but now they are being openly displayed.

Nowadays Weishaupt's secret objective is being openly proclaimed in Satanism – 'the overthrow of the government by revolutions and chaos!' Communism has the same goal, because both Communism and Satanism are fed by the same source of inspiration – hatred of Christ and the Christians. That explains the striking similarity between their plans and methods. The Communists were ordered to create chaos so as to seize the reins of government. While posing as peacemakers and heralding peace, they were to set the torch alight for the revolution. And beforehand they were to make the preparations by circulating large quantities of pornographic literature so as to destroy the moral fibre of the youth. As one of their mottoes runs, 'Corrupt the young, get them away from religion, fixate them with sex . . .'[26] They also smuggled in huge quantities of drugs – one way of breaking down the resistance of those outside their direct sphere of influence. All these measures were to lay the groundwork for the revolution and help the Communists attain their ends, for to them 'peace' is none other than Communist world dominion. This is a well-known fact about Communism.

But what does the Satanist LaVey say about his goals? In his opinion Satanism will lead to a totalitarian world government. In this police state the leaders would practise black magic; the weak members of society would be eliminated and Satanism made the state religion.[27] It is no surprise to hear that LaVey has the appropriate flag to fit these statements – the flag of the USSR – hanging in his lower chamber. Furthermore, books about Satanism are published by a Communist-run press and sold in large bookstores on the West Coast of America that are operated by the Communist Party.[28]

Thus, contrary to common opinion, Satanism is not merely 'underground religion'; it is highly political. The startling similarity of the philosophies of Satanists from Weishaupt to LaVey and Communists from Marx to Mao reveals their affinity. With the rapid pace of the end times, both ideologies hasten towards their ultimate goal of a Communist, Satanist world dictatorship.

By what means will this world state be established – this 'kingdom of peace', this pseudo-utopia of prosperity and justice? By peaceful means? What blessings and joys does this future world religion hold in store? Freedom from fears? True brotherly love? And who will be the object of worship in this religion? Iniquity breeds iniquity. The instigator is Satan who 'was a murderer from the beginning' (John 8:44). So it is impossible for him to create a kingdom of peace and paradise. Communism in its various forms has already shown its true self with the grotesque wholesale slaughtering of over 120 million lives; and now Satanism is beginning to lower its mask as well. Beneath it we see murder, carnage and sadism!

In Los Angeles the murder of a teacher caused a sensation. When her corpse was found, the heart, lungs and other parts of her body were missing. They were used for a sacrificial ceremony to the devil.[29] In another instance, a 21-year-old murderer told a criminal investigator, 'Satan's my master.' He cut off his victim's arms, legs, than ate his heart. A week later when he was arrested in Salinas, California, he was in possession of a Satanic Bible and several finger bones.[30]

In 1971 in New Jersey two boys killed a third at his request, for he said that Satan would bring him back to life as the leader of a legion of devils.[31] A young female Satanist, who 'swears she once saw the devil himself during a black ceremony, was convicted of manslaughter for stabbing a 62-year-old man to death. "I really enjoyed killing him," she said . . . in her Miami jail cell between elaborate rituals to Satan.'[32]

The notorious Manson 'family' who practised black magic and group sex made the headlines. They murdered seven whites in order to put the blame on the blacks; their fiendish scheme was to trigger off a revolutionary race war between blacks and whites. After this atrocious crime they sat down to eat dinner in the presence of their victims.[33]

In various cases of this type, the accused were tested by psychiatrists and found to be completely sane.

Does this give us a glimpse of a future world religion, when Communism and Satanism are united in the hatred of God? A student who visited a Church of Satan in California told us, 'At the entrance there was a mosaic of Christ on the floor. Everyone who entered the church had to step on it and spit on His face . . .'

That which should be preached from the pulpit comes, from a secular magazine instead. *Time*, for example, comments on the vile manifestations of the devil's cult, 'Recently history has shown terrifyingly enough that the demonic lies barely beneath the surface, ready to catch men unawares with new and more horrible manifestations . . .'[34]

The rise of the Church of Satan is an unmistakable sign of the times we are living in. The day has come when Communism and Satanism are achieving their common goals – revolution, chaos, persecution of Christians, the take-over of power, a world state, a world monetary system, a world government and a world religion.

Now for the first time Satanism, the religion based on hatred of God and His Son Jesus Christ, feels free to come out into the open. It is asserting its influence throughout the world, even making in-roads into television. These are all indications that a new era has dawned; the hand of the world clock has moved forward, and Jesus' prophecies for the last times have begun to be fulfilled. As we read in Scripture, 'You will be hated by all nations for my name's sake' (Matt. 24:9), and indeed Christians will soon be persecuted in all parts of the world. These are highly crucial times. The Satanic spirit that once took hold of Weishaupt, Robespierre and the Jacobins led to the blood bath of the French Revolution. Countless Christians ended their lives at the guillotine – but that was only in one country. At that time Satanism, which was behind it all, was kept a secret, whereas today this Satanic spirit holds sway almost all over the world. Consequently it will end in a blood bath of Christians throughout the world, which will be a thousand times more atrocious than that of the French Revolution.

The jigsaw pieces are beginning to fit together. Now it is obvious why strikes, revolts and riots are reported on all sides these days. Revolution – this one thought possesses every nation, whether it be China or Japan, the USSR, or the 'Christian' nations in the West such as France, Great Britain, Italy, West Germany, Finland, the Scandinavian countries, the United States and Canada, Australia, or the countries of Latin America and Africa. Institutions are undermined to a large extent by Communists and manipulated by revolutionary agents. In many cases the Communists have already assumed control, gaining more and more key positions in public life. Many brains are working for the official day of take-over, which can come either as a *coup d'état* or by 'legal means', i.e. by gaining a majority in parliament with a fraudulent manoeuvre. New governments, which are then formed, can remould society according to Marxist doctrine.

Where Is the Church Heading?

Do we still remember? In the mid sixties a strange silence fell upon the various Christian churches throughout the world on the subject of the world-wide strategy of Communism. A priest from Venezuela wrote, 'It seems to me as though shop-keepers are withdrawing from the window the goods that don't sell well at the moment. The Church is withdrawing her anti-Communism and the Communists, their anti-religiosity. The result has been confusion; and resistance has been weakened by the hope of peaceful co-existence, of dialogue and of a genuine renewal of the Church.'[35]

Never before in history has there been such a situation in the Church. In the course of time the attitude of the institutional church towards Communism and atheism has changed from that of mere silence to marked sympathy – a development which indicates that the world clock will soon strike midnight. The victory of Communism is imminent and Christian persecution is about to break out. Of course, in the Christian world there is no open talk of brotherhood with Communism; but the possibility of a humanistic world government is being discussed. A full-time worker of the World Council of Churches in Geneva spoke about the aims of this organization on October 28, 1972 on the West German television station SFB. 'The World Council of Churches . . . a possible model for a future world government.' The possibility of a universal church leading to a world government is being considered by others in the Protestant Church.

To achieve a syncretism of all religions and ideologies – including Communism – the Great Commission to preach the Gospel is being reduced to a mere 'dialogue' with the heathen religions. Reports about the World Mission Conference of the WCC early 1973 in Bangkok, Thailand, demonstrate this trend. In a preparatory document for this conference the programme director of the World Council of Churches in Geneva said, for instance, that the problem of dialogue meant learning to respect the work of the Holy Spirit in the whole world, not only within the realm of religion, but also within the secular beliefs and ideologies.[36]

At the Bangkok Conference even Maoism was presented several times as an acceptable, if not superior, alternative to Christianity. And the contribution of the Chinese Cultural Revolution to our understanding of 'salvation today' was discussed. The ultimate results of such dialogues with Marxists and Maoists are illustrated in a 'litany' of a modern version of the Beatitudes, which was cited in the report of Section I of the Bangkok Conference. 'You found all the traditional language meaningless and became "an atheist by the grace of God". I rejoice with you, my brother.'

Thus the decision of this conference comes as no surprise. The plenary session recommended that the churches in the West should refrain from sending missionaries to the Third World for the time being and to use the money saved, to support the liberation movements – that is, revolutionaries that advocate the use of violence. As early as 1969 at the Fourth Assembly of the World Council of Churches in Uppsala, Sweden this tendency could be seen clearly. As a guide and introduction to this assembly a brochure was published with the title, *Renewal in Mission*. This document freely used the great words of mission, but in radically new ways. For example, changing the social order by revolutionary methods (apparently heedless of what the revolutionaries believe about Jesus) was called reconciliation of man to God. Consequently, supporting a revolution in Brazil or Chile is regarded as mission. In a WCC book called *Salvation Today*, one article is entitled, 'Saved by Mao'.[37]

As early as 1966 Dr John C. Bennett, president of New York's influential Union Theological Seminary, a leading figure in the National and World Council of Churches, proposed that the West change its attitude towards China. 'The Chinese revolution . . . calls for awe initially rather than condemnation.' He continues, 'Communism needs to be seen as the instrument of modernization, of national unity, of greater social welfare.'[38] At the World Council of Churches Conference on the Church and Society, Red China was described as '. . . the new saviour of the poor nations of the world.'[39]

What attitude are Christians supposed to take? A universal church at the cost of truth and love? The World Council of Churches as pacemaker for a humanistic unified world state? Mao's aims and methods acceptable for Christian churches? Because the spiritual renewal of man and society does not appear to be successful any more, the support and advocation of violence are regarded as legitimate to attain renewal. Such views can only be held by a Church that has largely lost her Biblical foundation, her Christian hope and her relationship to the cross and to the resurrection of Jesus Christ, and now shares the ideals and methods of those who deny God and hate Christ.

Marx and Lenin tolerated 'Christian' ideas, if these seemed to further the cause of Communism and could help towards world conquest. If the church in general has such an antichristian spirit, she will turn into a godless world church. No doubt such a church in her initial as well as in her later stages will be convenient to a future world government opposed to Christianity. The Biblical prophecies in the Book of Revelation are beginning to be fulfilled: the Church is falling into a state of apostasy, becoming a harlot – and when the Antichrist appears, she will join forces with him (Rev. 17:1, 3).

What we are experiencing in the Protestant Church is also happening in the Roman Catholic Church. Her foundations have been undermined and her views have been partially altered, because the Communists have been to a large extent successful in infiltrating institutions. The seeds that were sown in secret by forerunners are now germinating for all to see. At their Eleventh Party Congress in 1964 the Communist Party of Italy made the following statement about the Second Vatican Council, '. . . A hitherto unforeseen opportunity has arisen. By making the right manoeuvre we can draw closer to the final victory . . . Free of charge the Vatican Council has placed the best means at our disposal to reach the Catholic public . . . The conditions were never so favourable for us.' Roman Catholics themselves write, 'The Pope is right; the devil has broken into the Church.'[40] In this case the apocalyptic signs are also evident.

It is nearly midnight and Christian persecution is on the threshold. Thus as Christians we cannot evade the issue. One question is important: 'Am I ready to suffer for Jesus and to lay down my life for Him?' Jesus' command, 'Be prepared!', is His summons to His disciples today. This command is like a trumpet call to startle us out of our sleep when we are too involved in the everyday affairs of life. The Lord wants us to practise now for tomorrow so that we can stand in the hour of trial. Yet many Christian groups, even those that realize the dangers of the current leftist trend in the institutional church, neglect their intensive spiritual training for the time of suffering, although we are standing on the brink of Christian persecution, and disaster is threatening the whole world. Looking through some of their magazines, one does not get the impression that we are living in a highly crucial era. Although some groups are concerned with the literal interpretation of the Bible, others with liturgical matters, and others with the charismatic experience, they are not gripped by the most important issue that will determine our destiny tomorrow. The sense of urgency is missing, as well as the fervent entreaty, "Lord, prepare us!"

What could be the explanation? In order to keep us from spiritual preparation the devil resorts to another method to lull us into a false state of security. A certain teaching, which prevails in many Christian groups, asserts that the believers will be raptured before the great revolutions, the persecution of Christians and the nuclear war. The more alarming the daily news becomes, the more this teaching is relied on. Thus countless numbers of believers are diverted from the real preparation – a life of contrition and repentance – which will make us ready for suffering, for the persecution of Christians and the world disaster that will follow.

Jesus said, 'If they persecuted me, they will persecute you' (John 15:20). In our present age His words are being fulfilled in lands under Communist rule and will be fulfilled in every new country that comes under their dominion. Why should we suppose that we can escape persecution? Jesus prophesied persecution for the end times, which we have now entered, when He said, 'You will be hated by all nations for my name's sake' (Matt. 24:9). The last times in particular are characterized by the hatred against believers, the blood of many martyrs and the severest Christian persecution in history. So let us not deceive ourselves and rest in false security and complacency, saying, As true believers, we shall be raptured before the persecution.'

Such notions come from the enemy. The Apostle Paul made it plain to the Church at Thessalonica, who expected the rapture to be earlier than it was due, that it could not possibly precede the time of suffering. 'Let no man deceive you by any means: for that day shall not come, except there come a falling away first, and that man of sin be revealed, the son of perdition' (2 Thess. 2:3 AV). Here the apostle is not referring to apostasy as a gradual development, a current trend, but in connection with a significant Antichristian personage who has not yet appeared. Furthermore, 1 Corinthians 15:51f. indicates that the believers will not be raptured to the Lord until the last trumpet is blown. That means they will have to live through the severe sufferings brought by the first six trumpet judgments, which have yet to come upon mankind (Rev. 8 and 9). However, this does not imply that these believers will have to endure the great tribulation during the Antichrist's reign.

But it is the suffering of the coming persecution that will prepare the Christians who survive, for the rapture. Although a disciple of Jesus lives in joyful expectation of the rapture, he realizes that only those who have walked with Jesus on the way of the cross will be caught up to meet Him in the air. Suffering had prepared them to meet the Lord and behold Him in His glory, for no one can see God without holiness (Heb. 12:14). Suffering alone transforms them and brings them great glory; neither conversion nor baptism in the Holy Spirit is a guarantee for the rapture.

Jesus' summons applies to our times more than ever before. 'Be on your guard! Prepare yourselves!' By the time persecution breaks out, we must be ready to meet suffering – everything depends on that. So let us prepare to suffer; let us surrender ourselves ever anew, dedicating ourselves to suffering.

And we shall be prepared by

Constantly renewing our trust in the heavenly Father,

Surrendering our will to God ever anew,

Keeping our eyes fixed on Jesus,

Resisting sin and fighting the battle of faith daily,
Realizing the privilege of suffering for Christ,

Remembering our vocation to make up what is lacking in Christ's afflictions for the sake of His Body.

Love
Prepares to
Suffer

Trust God for Today and Tomorrow

Let us be realistic about the future. When persecution of Christians breaks out in our lands, will any one of us be able to remain faithful to the end? Judging by our own strength and resources, we are forced to conclude that we are incapable of bearing such suffering. However, by approaching the matter from another angle, we are filled with triumphant assurance for the future. There is another factor to remember that will tip the scales in our favour: the omnipotence of our heavenly Father. We must include Him in our calculations, for He possesses all the strength we lack and will demonstrate His power when we undergo persecution.

This calls for a complete change in our way of thinking. We must discard all idea of relying on ourselves, since from the very outset it is obvious that our power of endurance will not suffice in suffering. But there is Someone who will stand by our side, demonstrate His might and lend us aid in future trials – God our Father, and everything hinges on whether or not we reckon with Him. His power is so immense that our ability to suffer grows insignificant by comparison. It makes no difference whether we have great or little power of endurance or none at all, for to God it is the same, whether He has to impart much or little of His strength to us. Indeed, He was referring to the weak when He promised, 'My power is made perfect in weakness' (2 Cor. 12:9).

Today we must practise claiming His aid for ourselves. When we can no longer see a way out of our predicament, we must reckon alone with God and His assistance, for He has given us a definite pledge of help. His name is Yea and Amen, and He will be faithful to His promises so that in the midst of persecution and suffering we shall experience the truth of His words, 'I will never fail you nor forsake you' (Heb. 13:5). 'Fear not, for I am with you . . . I will strengthen you, I will help you, I will uphold you with my victorious right hand' (Isa. 41:10). We only have to do our part by claiming the promise. And this we do by translating faith into action and coming to God our Father in every sorrow and saying to Him,

'Abba, dearest Father, I trust You.
You will uphold me and carry me through.
You are with me; You bring me the help I need.
I take refuge in Your heart.
When I am united with You, nothing can harm me.
You are my Shield, and Your angels watch over me.'

Whenever fear grips our hearts as we think of the coming persecution, let us repeat this prayer:

'My Father,
From the foundations of the world You have ordained what will happen to me every day, every hour during persecution. You know me; You know my character, my capabilities. You know whether I am weak or strong, and before sending

anything into my life, You measure it first according to my strength.

Your loving heart sees to it that I am not tried beyond my strength in the trials and testings during persecution – of that I can rest assured. My Father, if anyone has evil intentions for me, You only have to speak a word and his attempts are foiled. My tormentors can never do more to me than You permit. And Jesus will give me the strength to endure.

Lord Jesus, take my life. I want to suffer and even die for You out of love and gratitude, for You have loved me and brought me salvation through Your agonizing death on the cross.'

If we draw near to God in deep trust, we shall experience His help. But there is a condition to fulfil. We must come to the Father as true children with humble and contrite hearts. In other words we must lie at His feet, humbled beneath our sin. Ever anew we must confess our sin to Him and before men, making a complete break with it. Grace is promised to such penitent sinners. God inclines Himself to the humble and helps them, but He opposes the proud and self-righteous. It is vastly important that we bring our sins into the light and receive forgiveness through Jesus' blood, before the time of suffering and persecution comes upon us! Then God will stand by us and let us experience His fatherly help.

In times of persecution the Father Himself will take charge of the situation – and not we – for He has pledged Himself to intervene on our behalf. Indeed miracles will happen and the Biblical events of long ago will become present-day occurrences for us. When God intervenes, torture will have no effect. Night after night in an unheated cell a girl was made to sleep on the cold cement floor, according to a recent account from White Russia. It was winter time and she had no outer garment to keep her warm. Yet as she testified, 'Every night when I lay down in that icy grave, I committed myself into the hands of God and – it was a miracle! – a warm current of air surrounded me all night long and I could rest well.'[41] This was obviously God's doing!

When God intervenes, riotous gangs and terrorists advancing on us will not be able to cause us any harm. But when the time comes for some of us to lay down our lives for Jesus, after having experienced many instances of protection and deliverance, we shall encounter another miracle of God – as in the case of Stephen, the first Christian martyr. God let him see into the open heavens. The stoning could not drive Stephen to despair. On the contrary, he was filled with divine joy and 'his face was like the face of an angel' (Acts 6:15).

Some years ago there was a moving testimony from the persecuted Church in China. An elder of a small church was taken to court because of his faith in Christ. He was beaten brutally and thrown into prison, but after a few days he was released for no apparent reason. At the next worship service, he gave his testimony to the assembled church, which had been praying for him without ceasing during his imprisonment. 'When I received the 240 lashes, I thought of Stephen and how he was stoned. Then I had an experience similar to his. Above me I could see the Lord Jesus for whom I was suffering, and I was comforted beyond words. It was as though a hand was laid upon my mangled back so that I no longer felt the pain. In addition the Lord told me that I would be set free in a few days, and that really did happen, as you can all see.' His eyes still shone with the Lord's comfort and on him rested the invisible aureole of honour and glory – won by those who have suffered disgrace for Jesus' sake.[42]

Once long ago God uttered a command and out of nothing He formed heaven and earth, a marvellous creation. The same God who lives today needs say but a word and that which would normally cause us agony or injury is rendered ineffective. Five hours long, night after night, a young soldier, thinly clad, was made to stand outside in the freezing cold ($-20°$ F.). Humanly speaking, he should have contracted a serious illness or have died; yet nothing of the sort happened to this soldier, suffering for Jesus' sake. Another time he was deprived of nourishment for five days, but the Lord sustained and strengthened him. God proved Himself to be a God of miracles. This was the testimony of the Russian soldier, Vanya Mojsejev, of our times.[43]

God speaks a word and there is action. He intervenes and grants us help when we cry to Him in our need, as this young Baptist martyr did. God the Father, who does not forget the young ravens that cry, does not forget any of His children when they call upon Him. His attention is especially drawn to those who are suffering out of love for Him and are in fear and dire distress. He cannot forget them or leave them without comfort, without help, since

43

that would contradict His very nature which is love –
and God cannot deny Himself. Our heavenly Father
is Love and at the same time He is the Almighty;
He acts according to His nature, treating us with
love and exercising His omnipotence on our behalf
just as He has promised.

Thus one of the watchwords for this preparatory
time when we are faced with problems and suffering
is, 'Pray! Hasten to the Father!' God is waiting
for His child to come so that He can help him. So let
us implore the Father to help, and rush to His arms,
for they are strong and will carry us through. Then
we shall be practised by the time persecution comes.
When we are in extreme anguish and misery, we may
not be able to formulate long prayers, but then we
only have to say, 'My Father, I trust You!' Let us
say this prayer over and over again; it contains power
and brings us help, for we receive according to our
trust. Either God will avert the plight or we shall
experience His loving presence so wonderfully that we
are oblivious to the horror about us.

We can really place our trust in the Father, for He
is worthy of our implicit trust. God our Father in
Jesus Christ has not only shown His love in words;
He has proved it in action. Although we have bur-
dened and wearied Him with our sins, grieved Him and
caused Him suffering and so often rebelled against
Him, He sacrificed His Son for our sakes – an act
which caused Him immeasurable anguish. The
Father's love and faithfulness have been tried and
proven; they are absolutely reliable. And His love
does not change; His heart is the same today.

Long ago He made the supreme sacrifice of His

only Son – as proof of His love – in order to save us and re-open heaven for us. And now He wishes to lavish His love upon those who are no longer His enemies but His adopted children who have come to love Him as their Father. His love will come down in cascades upon His children, particularly when they are undergoing suffering and persecution for Jesus' sake. He will pour out His heart of love upon them in their grief and pain, turning hell into heaven. Many of His own, suffering for His name's sake, have had this experience during the years spent in the diabolical conditions of concentration camps. Father Kentenich, who was imprisoned in the concentration camp of Dachau for four years during World War II, gave the following testimony there at a memorial service. 'Dachau was not hell for us, but rather heaven. How often we said that to each other then! For what is heaven but the deep fellowship of love with the Triune God and with those who love Him!'[44]

Knit to His Will, We Are Strong

When the mob came to take Jesus prisoner, He met them with the words, 'I am he!', thus giving Himself into their hands. Jesus was prepared to suffer, to be imprisoned, to be tried and scourged, since His will was knit to the Father's. Being at one with the will of God makes us strong in the hour of deepest affliction, even if commandos should come to arrest us too. Being at one with God means having a covenant with the almighty, immortal God, who contends for us. Being united with Jesus Christ means having the victorious, risen Lord at our side, the Lord over all things and all men, before whom all powers and dominions must yield. When we are united with the Almighty, we shall be able to master every situation. This union with God is essential for the time of persecution, but it has to be practised now, for unity with God, which means unity with His will, does not come to us naturally.

So often our will clashes with God's. His ways and leadings oppose our natural inclinations. We find it hard to accept His will. We find it hard to submit to those who insult us or act against our personal wishes and opinions. We protest and rebel, thus defying the will of God. And because our unity with God is broken, our strength to overcome in suffering is also broken. When our will revolts against God's will, a barrier is erected between God and us, and we have to undergo the painful experience of having God against us, for 'God opposes the proud', who set their wills against His.

We shall have to pay the consequences during the great persecution for each time we have defied God's will and leadings by asserting our own wishes and will instead. In the hour of testing we shall be weak. And the reverse is equally true. We shall be rewarded for every time we have consented to the will of God and said, 'Yes, Father!', when faced with the trials and vexations of everyday life, or our personal sorrows and troubles. The dedication of the will binds us more and more tightly to God, cementing a union that will hold in persecution and torment. When we are united with God, nothing can harm us.

This prayer, 'Yes, Father!', must become like second nature to us by the time persecution breaks out. We must start training ourselves now, so that every time our heart produces a No to God's leadings, it will be turned into a Yes. It is vital that we declare war on the spirit of defiance that arises in our heart when our will is thwarted. We must learn to submit to others, since it is ultimately God who ordains the course of life. This must all take place now – on the eve of persecution. So let us pray, 'By the time persecution comes, let my will be completely knit to Your will through repeated commitments to suffering.'

But who can surrender his will unconditionally to the will of God? Who is able to say, 'Yes, Father!' ever anew, even when it demands his life, his all? Only he who bears the true image of God in his heart and declares who God is. God is Love; His will is goodness; His thoughts, purposes and decisions come from a fatherly heart which is brimming over with love. He has only the best intentions for us, His children, even though we may not understand His actions. In beholding the Father's heart, we are moved to repeat the prayer, 'Yes, Father!', no matter how hard we find His leadings; and in time this prayer will knit us to the will of God completely, evoking in us the response of love so that we welcome suffering.

It is absolutely essential that our wills be at one with the will of God, for otherwise we shall not be steadfast in the coming time of persecution. If we are only sometimes committed to God's will in situations and relationships when our will is frustrated, we shall have only a loose connection with God – and that will not suffice. A wall made of loose bricks will collapse when a storm breaks out. In order to withstand the storm, the bricks must be cemented together and the same principle applies to our lives. By taking advantage of the countless opportunities today for making great or small commitments of the will, our union with God will become sturdy and unshakeable. Then during affliction we shall be united with our loving Father in His omnipotence and with our Lord Jesus Christ, who is the mightiest of all. As Lord and God, Jesus has only to speak a word and a prison door will swing open, a trial will take a direction in our favour, and medications and drugs intended to weaken our resistance and make us pliable cannot harm us. And at cross-examinations the Holy Spirit, the Spirit of wisdom, will help us, inspiring us with the right words. Indeed, when we are knit to the will of God, we are invincible, for His will is stronger than any other will; all must submit to Him.

In the midst of persecution we shall rest in the Father's arms like a child. The wickedness of others, the torture and suffering they plan to inflict upon us cannot harm us. When we are knit to God, we are strong and shall be able to endure persecution just as the martyrs did in past centuries. Current reports from Communist countries testify that Christians suffering torture receive supernatural strength. 'I feel better than ever! The joy of the Lord is our strength,' wrote Aida Skripnikova, a young woman, after her second term in a Russian prison camp. She derives her strength from committing herself to the will of God.

'Abide in me, and I in you' (John 15:4). If we are united with Christ, it does not matter what trouble or danger befalls us. For, 'who shall separate us from the love of Christ? Shall tribulation, or distress, or persecution, or famine, or nakedness, or peril, or sword?' None of these, for we can answer triumphantly, 'I am sure that neither death, nor life, nor angels, nor principalities, nor things present, nor things to come, nor powers, nor height, nor depth, nor anything else in all creation, will be able to separate us from the love of God in Christ Jesus our Lord' (Rom. 8:35, 38f.).

Immersed in Jesus, We Are Invincible

What does the future hold? Before us we can see people tormented in body, soul and spirit. We can see the revolutionary mobs breaking into houses, dragging away the Christians and torturing them. The mere thought of the Satanic darkness that is about to engulf us is petrifying. This is precisely what Satan hopes to achieve, for he is the instigator of this persecution of Christians. A person crippled with fear is incapable of engaging in spiritual warfare and so will never win the victory. Moreover when he undergoes suffering and torture for Jesus' sake, he will be unable to overcome.

We must be strong for the time of persecution and, indeed, we shall be invincible, if we have the right perspective. We are always influenced by what we look at. Thus it is important that we tear our eyes away from scenes of horror, hatred and evil that are inspired by the powers of darkness. If we dwell only upon the coming horrors, picturing them in detail, we are lost. The horror will overcome us and drag us down into the quicksands of despair. We must turn our eyes away altogether and set our gaze on Jesus Christ, the Prince of Victory, who has destroyed the works of the devil and hell, and continues to do so. Victorious might emanates from Jesus, imparting strength to us and making us steadfast. Our only means of deliverance now, and later when our lives are jeopardized, is to gaze at Him.

The most amazing things take place when we turn our eyes upon Jesus; comfort is poured into our fearful hearts now and later during persecution. One glance at our Saviour and Helper transforms us and our situation. In particular the sight of our Lord suffering and in disgrace, crowned with thorns, implants in our souls the desire to suffer. His infinite love is revealed to us as we gaze at Him in His suffering. But if our hearts and minds are not filled with Jesus' sufferings, we cannot suffer for Him. Today more than ever we must meditate on His sufferings; then we shall come very close to Him and our own suffering will seem small.

Jesus implores us, 'Look at Me when the horror is about to swallow you. Then the darkness which has entered your soul and is gathering round you will be turned into light.' His countenance is like the radiant sun, sending forth rays of light that fall upon our hearts, transforming darkness into light.

We have to confront the future. Indeed, Jesus warns us by saying, 'Watch! Be alert!' In other words He tells us to realize the significance of the present age, and to recognize the signs of the time. The sole purpose of recognizing that darkness has fallen is to take advantage of the time left before persecution breaks out. Now on the eve of persecution we must practise seeking Jesus ever anew with the inner eye of faith.

His is the loveliest countenance of all, illuming the whole universe. When our eyes rest upon His countenance, we are charged with power. When we are in deepest distress and suffering, Jesus turns His radiant gaze upon us and our hearts are comforted. If we look to Jesus, allowing Him to enthral us, our hearts will be immersed in divine peace and joy.

The right perspective will save us during persecution and suffering. But we have only a short time to practise. The way we approach our everyday trials and problems casts the die for later. Today it is vital that we see beyond these problems, not worrying about them, not getting too involved in them, or letting them cripple us and weigh us down. We must turn our eyes away from these problems and look to Jesus, the Ruler of heaven and earth. Then He will grant us help. He gazes at us lovingly, promising us, 'I will help you.' When the hour of darkness has struck, He reveals His countenance even more, letting His infinite love, glory and power shine upon us in our night – this we can count on.

As we fasten our eyes on His countenance, we drink in the love emanating from His features and experience His help. Rapt in His gaze, we are no longer haunted by the faces of our tormentors; we are oblivious to the horror, the terrible conditions. Jesus alone, our Lord and King, fills our hearts, and we experience the power that comes from beholding Him, our suffering and victorious Lord.

In His love Jesus looks at us, waiting for us to return His gaze and to fix our eyes upon Him in the midst of anguish and distress. His name is a great source of power and He waits for us to pronounce it as we behold Him: 'Jesus, my Helper. Jesus, my Saviour. Jesus, my Bridegroom.' In the minor sorrows and troubles of our present-day life we must learn to look to Him and call upon His name. We must escape from the vicious circle where we revolve round ourselves and our problems, and meditate on His sufferings instead. Then our suffering will grow insignificant. We must trust His promises of love, help and power, and as we look to Him, calling upon His victorious name, we shall be delivered from the quicksands of despair. Our souls are restored as we behold Him and we have the comforting assurance of His presence.

Someone stands beside me, I am not alone;
Someone shares my suffering and sorrow unknown –
Jesus, my Helper and Victor.

Trained in Spiritual Warfare

During this short time on earth everything depends on our overcoming in the persecution of Christians, the hour of great trial, which is about to come upon us. We must stand the test of suffering, and our faith must prove itself in the furnace of affliction, since the outcome will decide our eternal destiny. During persecution Satan will make his assault on us with the torment that fiendish men inflict upon us. He intends to defeat us and rob us of our heavenly crown. In order to carry out this plan he will attack us at our weak points and work on our sinful inclinations, such as fear of suffering, cowardice, rebellion, disloyalty to our convictions out of fear of causing offence or incurring disapproval, dependence upon the praise and love of others or false emotional attachments to people. When persecution breaks out, it will become obvious how much we fought against our sins – how seriously we took them and to what extent we overcame them. We shall not be spared the consequences if we were so taken up with the trivial mundane affairs, the sorrows and joys of 'today', that we forgot the 'morrow'. The 'morrow' will bring persecution, and no one can stand this test unless he has prepared himself in advance, by fighting an earnest battle against sin, in faith in Jesus' redemption.

God has commanded us to lay aside every sin that

clings to us and weighs us down (Heb. 12:1). Why? Sin weakens us. Normally if we are bound to others, dependent on their praise and love, over-anxious to please, or afraid of causing offence or incurring disapproval, we shall not be able to remain steadfast during cross-examinations. Bondage to people and to things of this world actually binds us to Satan, bringing us into his clutches. And as a result we weaken and succumb. Then we are even capable of denying Jesus, thus forfeiting our eternal heritage in glory.

The Book of Revelation refers to the persecuted Christians in the last times, saying, 'They have conquered him [Satan] by the blood of the Lamb . . .' (Rev. 12:11). But when do we use the word 'conquer'? Only when a battle is involved, for there is no victory without a battle. And when are we willing to fight the battle of faith so as to be freed from our slavery to sin? Only when we refuse to tolerate our sins, such as quarrelsomeness, thirst for power, the gratification of our desires, envy, self-will, untruthfulness – and really hate them. Only when we realize that such sinning is a grievous offence against God and man, do we seek release at any price. Then we are willing to fight against our sins to the point of shedding blood; then we are willing to fight this battle now in preparation for the future.

The crucial question for the time of suffering and persecution is 'Will sin still be able to weaken me then to the extent it does now? Or shall I be able to overcome in persecution, having fought against my sins beforehand?' We shall be prepared to suffer, if we have fought this battle now in the time of preparation.

Only if we have let the blood of Jesus release us now from our bondage to food and sleep, and ease and comfort, will we be strong enough to bear hunger, thirst and physical suffering. We shall be able to bear our tormentors and betrayers in patience and love, and to forgive them, if we have overcome all bitterness, irreconciliation and rebellion now in our everyday lives. Then we shall be experienced soldiers and Satan will not be able to defeat us in the hour of testing.

Now is the time for practice. Jesus' admonition to build our house upon rock and not upon sand, so that it will stand in the impending storm, is highly relevant for us (Matt. 7:21-27). When the flood comes, only that which has a firm foundation will not be swept away. Thus it is not our knowledge about Christianity that counts, but the way we live. We must live according to Jesus' words, doing the will of God and not just saying, 'Lord! Lord!' His will is our sanctification (1 Thess. 4:3); and sanctification does not imply holiness – that is, flawlessness in the perfectionist sense of the word. Sanctification is a process that includes fighting the battle of faith against sin with our last ounce of strength so that we may be remoulded into Jesus' image.

In this battle of faith we must take the right measures. 'If your right eye causes you to sin, pluck it out and throw it away' (Matt. 5:29). In other words we have to take action, confessing our sins to God, and also to our fellow men whom we repeatedly wrong. We need to humble ourselves before them, to admit our guilt and say those vital words ever anew, 'Please forgive me; I am very sorry.'

57

Do we yield to our sinful inclinations? Have we formed false attachments to others? Are we bound to our hobbies or money? Are we addicted to tranquillizers, sedatives or other drugs? Are we on bad terms with anyone? Are we envious? Or are we so egoistic that we cannot bear to be disturbed? If so, we must take the appropriate measures. There must be an 'about face' in our lives and we must give God a token of our willingness, an indication that our desire to become free is in earnest, though, of course, only Jesus can bring us release from our sinful bondages. And we shall discover, 'If the Son makes you free, you will be free indeed' (John 8:36).

Every time we look to Jesus in faith, every time we pray to Him in faith, our fetters are loosened some more; but we must also humble ourselves beneath His hand, submitting patiently to His chastening, and persevering in faith in His victory until we experience release. This persevering faith turns us into overcomers, so that we shall be able to stand firm even during persecution.

We must fight against our sins to the point of shedding blood, taking practical steps to overcome them. In particular we must gain the victory over the sins of cowardice and the fear of men – conformity, the desire to please others, and disloyalty to our convictions out of fear of incurring disapproval or causing offence. During persecution it is vital that we are able to bear witness to Jesus. And only if we practise making an uncompromising stand for Jesus now, will we be able to do so in perilous times. Today, when God Himself is being attacked and blasphemy has reached unheard-of proportions, the challenge to make a stand for the Lord is all the more urgent. Jesus is being subjected to the most outrageous indignities, mockery and degradation, while all sorts of obscenities are attributed to Him as an excuse for man's wickedness. He is presented as a clown, a simpleton, and portrayed as seen through the eyes of Judas. The prospect of a 'blasphemous, sadistic and pornographic' film about Jesus shows to what lengths man dares to go in blaspheming the Holy One of God.

Are we making a stand for Jesus? Do we voice our opposition when Jesus is treated this way? Today this is the question we are being asked. Witnessing means having the courage to be called 'old fashioned' or 'pharisaical' and thus humiliated. A true witness never remains silent or conforms to the crowd for the sake of being thought tolerant, sophisticated, understanding, broad-minded or modern.

This battle against our false sense of brotherly love, false emotional ties and dependence upon the opinions and approval of others becomes increasingly essential the closer persecution draws towards us. Then we shall need to take a stand against a universal church that does not recognize Jesus' act of redemption but embraces all religions and ideologies. The same applies, should we be confronted with a one and only permitted Bible, which gives a distorted version of the crucifixion, omitting all reference to the sacrificial atonement for sin, and presenting social reform as the only true gospel. Then we will be faced with this question: 'Do we love our Lord more than our own lives? Are we willing to lay them down for Him?' We cannot be alert enough to withstand the Satanic attempts to lull us to sleep and to lure us into a haze of confusion. Vigilance is essential. Now is the time to resist these attacks and to fight against sin, especially cowardice, conformity and the false concept of brotherly love. Then God will do everything to help us be victorious during persecution. And later we shall join the overcomers in heaven who 'have conquered him [Satan] . . . by the word of their testimony, for they loved not their lives even unto death' (Rev. 12:11).

The Privilege of Suffering for Christ

Christian persecution looms before us. It will probably exceed all previous ones in proportion and brutality – a fact which is enough to terrify us. Brainwashing, torture, concentration camps come to mind – the most terrible suffering, torment and even martyrdom. Yet there is a wonderful secret about this suffering, for it is quite different from the other afflictions that may come upon us. It is suffering 'for Christ'.

We are not suffering for some cause, nor for a mortal man with his shortcomings and delusive ideals, which he sets before us. We are not suffering for the sake of a ruler who deludes his subjects, perhaps even torturing them, as is frequently the case. History repeats itself, and to this very day thousands commit themselves to such leaders, not stopping at any sacrifice and even prepared to die for them, only to discover later that they had been deceived. As Christians, however, we have the wonderful privilege of suffering and giving our lives for the one Lord Jesus Christ during persecution. He is the Lord Most High, majestic and triumphant. As the Son of God robed in splendour, emanating love, righteousness and truth, He is unique. The greatest man on earth cannot compare with Him. He is altogether different, without sin. He is the Almighty, the Ruler of heaven and earth. In His amazing love for us He took the lowest place of all, letting Himself be despised by all mankind.

For our sakes He became the Man of Sorrows, voluntarily undergoing the most agonizing death. And once more today as the humble, meek Lamb of God he patiently endures the blasphemy, allowing Himself to be abused, mocked and utterly degraded in countless sacrilegious musicals, plays and other productions. Today Jesus calls us to His side more than ever before to suffer disgrace, contempt and persecution with Him. Let us give Him the response of our love, for He is worthy of it.

It is truly remarkable that sinful men are privileged to suffer for the Lord Jesus. After His sacrifice on the cross where He vanquished Satan, Jesus majestically led away the principalities and powers of the underworld as captives in a triumphal march. And soon He will openly display and manifest His victory over Satan before all the world! What a privilege it is to be able to suffer for this Lord of lords! With the breath of His mouth He will destroy the Antichrist and then establish His everlasting kingdom, where every knee will bow to Him and every tongue confess that Jesus Christ is Lord. In this kingdom the martyrs and overcomers will have the honour of reigning with Him for ever and ever. It is inconceivable that as sinful, mortal beings we are permitted to be 'God's fellowworkers' in serving Him and in paving the way for the eternal Kingdom of God, which is about to come. Yet it is utterly amazing that by our suffering we are also to be 'fellow-workers with God' and thus partners with Christ our Lord, who built His kingdom upon suffering. To suffer for Jesus and to help establish the Kingdom of God as 'a chosen instrument' – this was Paul's election. This calling was confirmed by the

Lord when He said, 'I will show him how much he must suffer for the sake of my name' (Acts 9:16).

Early Christian martyrs, as well as twentieth-century martyrs, were conscious of the tremendous honour of not only believing in Jesus but of suffering for Him. Paul considered it an act of grace, a privilege (Phil. 1:29 *The Living Bible*). In times of persecution those who suffered martyrdom were usually filled with a joy that was not of this world. Because their hearts were set on fire for Jesus, they were overwhelmed at the honour of bearing shame and disgrace and many hardships for His name's sake. To them the name of Jesus represented all glory and might, wisdom and beauty, and immeasurable love. His name always sounded in their hearts as the sweetest name.

Only because Jesus was their first and foremost Love, could the martyrs of recent years, like those of the past, endure persecution and suffering for Jesus joyfully and wholly surrendered to God. Even before persecution had broken out, love constrained them to share their Lord's pathway; they could not do otherwise. And Jesus' earthly life, even before His Passion began, was characterized by lowliness, humiliation, disappointments, poverty, loneliness, insults, rejection, many acts of self-denial, and sacrificial deeds. Those who had previously chosen Jesus' pathway for their own out of love for Him walked in His footsteps as true disciples so that by the time persecution came, they were practised in suffering and aflame with love for Him. The more they practised bearing their cross with Jesus, the closer they were knit to Him and the more fiercely blazed the fire of their love.

Jesus loves us tenderly and desires our love in

return. He entreats us, 'Give Me your love! Choose My way! Come, join Me! Take up your cross and follow Me!'

Today there is still time to practise true discipleship of the cross in order to be trained in suffering for the time of persecution. Jesus appeals to us with greater urgency than ever before, since our future depends on whether or not we follow Him now on the way of the cross. Today He is challenging us to set foot on His pathway and to deny ourselves and endure lowliness, humiliation, rejection, insults, injustice, disappointments, and bodily suffering out of love and dedication to Him. If we are willing to continue this path out of love for Him in spite of the cuts and bruises we receive on the way, if we say, 'For You, with You, Lord Jesus', our love will grow strong and we shall gain practice in suffering.

This is a gradual process. When we commit ourselves to the future suffering, the first stage of self-surrender is to say, 'Lord Jesus, as Your disciple I *must* suffer for You!' By the second stage we are able to say, 'I *want* to suffer for You!' But by the third stage we can say, 'It is a *privilege* to suffer for You; it is an honour to be counted worthy of this.' Let us constantly make new acts of dedication in order to reach this third stage, which is our goal of faith. During persecution we shall reap the fruits of this time of practice, and the bitterness of suffering will be turned into triumphant joy. 'The Lord Jesus has suffered so much on my behalf. Now I can show Him my love by suffering for Him.'

This triumphant joy and thanksgiving for the privilege of suffering for Jesus can be found in the letter from the Evangelical Christian Baptists of Russia, which they sent to all the churches in the world. At the second congress of their church council in 1970, these Baptists, the relatives of persecuted Christians, came together. Did they want to make an accusation? To complain of their suffering? To join in sorrowing for their fellow Christians who had been taken prisoner? Or to ask for release? On the contrary, the letter reads, 'We have come together – fathers, mothers, sons and daughters of prisoners – to thank the Lord for our suffering for Christ.'[45]

Suffering for Christ? Frequently – perhaps at night – we picture the horror, the bloodshed of the impending revolution, the persecution of Christians and the torture and anguish it will bring. But when this frightening darkness seeks to oppress us, our hearts can suddenly be filled with light. Two little words can effect total transformation, 'For Christ!' Fear of the future and of the torment in persecution is turned into comfort, peace and even triumphant joy when we look at Jesus, our Lord and Saviour, the Bridegroom of our souls. It is our privilege and desire to suffer for Jesus, who is eternal Joy, the Glory of heaven and earth, the sole Love of those who belong to Him.

In view of the coming suffering let us embrace the Lord Jesus with all our hearts and then we shall become joyful in our present fears and later in torment, for our hearts will be ringing with those blessed words, 'For You, Jesus, for You!' There is an account of the Baltic Professor of Theology, Traugott Hahn, when he was in captivity. Before his execution in 1919 the guards forced him to carry a pail of human excrement down the corridor. Seeing him so degraded,

Bishop Platon of the Orthodox Church, who was a fellow-prisoner, whispered to him, '*Radi Christa*' ('for the sake of Christ').[46] These words contain a wonderful hidden power. When the Presbyter Peter Wiens in Russia was about to be deported to a prison camp, he said good-bye to his wife with the words, '*Radi Christa*', not knowing whether he would ever see her again. These words set his wife at peace and strengthened his son – as the latter testified – when later he too was deported.[47]

The true image of Jesus never shines so brightly as in times of persecution when He manifests the greatness and power of His fervent love as He visits those suffering imprisonment for His sake. Cold cells, impregnated with horror, are transformed by Jesus' presence into a heavenly palace as the Dutch priest, Dr Titus Brandsma, testified in a poem which he wrote in a Gestapo prison where he was held captive in World War II:

> To suffer takes no special fortitude –
> But only love. All suffering seems good;
> For through it I become, O Lord, like You
> And suffering brings me to Your kingdom too.
>
> Indeed, all suffering is joy and gain,
> For out of love I sense no more the pain.
> It truly seems a high and glorious call,
> For it unites me with the Lord of all.
>
> Yes, let me be imprisoned and forlorn
> In icy-cold and dismal cell, alone,
> With no one else to help or comfort me;
> I'll never tire of this serenity.

If only You will stay with me, O Lord;
You've never been so close to me before.
O stay, my Jesus! Stay, Belovèd, here,
For all is well, if only You are near.[48]

Even children who suffer persecution come into a
deeper relationship with Jesus, who stays at their
side. They discover the reality of Jesus and the hidden
glory, the privilege, the honour of being considered
worthy to suffer for His name's sake. 'What is your
suffering for Jesus?' a ten-year-old boy asked a
Christian visiting a church in the Soviet Union while
on vacation. This boy had stayed in a camp with his
brothers and sisters during the years that his parents
were imprisoned because of their faith. However,
children and parents both left the camps with their
faith deepened as a result of the suffering. And now
the all-important question for this boy was whether a
believer had suffered for Jesus already. In his youthful
heart he no doubt sensed that suffering for Jesus was
an honour – a privilege.[49]

But not until we reach heaven and see the shining
crowns on the heads of those who patiently bore their
suffering, shall we fully realize what a privilege it is
to suffer for Jesus.

Who can measure the great treasure
Suffering and grief have brought?
Who has sight and understanding
For the good that pain has wrought?

Who may live there close to Jesus
In unending glory bright?
Those who shared the cross beside Him.
With the Lamb endured dark night.[50]

'Blessed are you when men hate you, and when they exclude you and revile you, and cast out your name as evil, on account of the Son of man! Rejoice in that day, and leap for joy, for behold, your reward is great in heaven' (Luke 6:22f.). A wonderful reward lies in store – and soon, very soon, suffering will be turned into eternal glory and immeasurable joy.

What greater privilege could there be than to suffer for Jesus, who wants to recompense our sufferings with a divine reward and eternal glory! Let us lift up our eyes to heaven – for one thought of heaven drives all earthly suffering away.

The Marvellous Purposes of God

'I rejoice in my sufferings for your sake,' the Apostle Paul declares in one of his letters (Col. 1:24). He realizes the privilege of making up in his own person whatever is still lacking in Christ's afflictions for the sake of His Body, which is the Church. Paul rejoices, since he knows that his suffering will have far-reaching effects for the Church. Through his suffering Paul is privileged to help carry out God's plan of salvation – an amazing thought! He is drawn into God's marvellous purposes for the Body of Christ.

What a tremendous commission has been entrusted to sinful man! Our suffering for Jesus' sake will yield wonderful fruit. This knowledge, this thought will help us to remain steadfast in the sufferings of persecution. We are not merely enduring the suffering that has been laid upon us, submitting to it with a 'Yes, Father!' Far more is involved. We are suffering for a definite purpose, for Christ and His Body, the Church. Jesus, the Lamb of God, gave His life as a sacrifice so that God's wonderful plan of salvation for the Church, and later for the whole of creation and for all nations, could be fulfilled. By contributing our suffering we help to complete these eternal purposes of God. This is our amazing privilege, for with our suffering we help to prepare the Church, the bride of the Lamb, and so hasten the day of Jesus' return.

We are living in the last times and this great day will come soon when God's plan for the Church, the bride of the Lamb, will be fulfilled. Thus the persecution of Christians in the end times is highly significant, for the last measure of suffering must be added before the bride of the Lamb can be completed in number and reach perfection. The overcomers in heaven will be longing for this day of fulfilment and thus waiting for us to take our part in suffering. Probably the marriage feast of the Lamb is already in preparation and all heaven is waiting for the bride. On that day of immeasurable joy and glory one of the goals in God's plan of salvation will be attained, and we may help to bring about this momentous event by contributing our share in suffering. This prospect makes suffering worthwhile for the present-day martyrs and gives them the strength to be steadfast. And when the marriage feast of the Lamb begins, all the kingdoms of this world will finally fall into the Lord's possession.

What a privilege and a high calling to suffer with Jesus! What an act of grace, what a special honour! Jesus, who on Calvary completed His sacrifice, who redeemed the whole world, waits in humility for the members of His Body to suffer with Him and for Him. They have the privilege of contributing their share of suffering so that His plan of salvation for mankind and the whole universe can be carried out. Suffering contains tremendous power, yielding abundant fruit, and it ends in victory, glory and resurrection.

This knowledge gives us the courage to lay down our lives for Jesus in the time of persecution. Suffering brings great blessing to others, for as the Apostle Paul said, 'I endure everything for the sake of the elect, that they also may obtain the salvation which in Christ Jesus goes with eternal glory' (2 Tim. 2:10). When persecution does break out, we have the privilege of suffering for our church or fellowship or for certain people, so that they may be saved, learn to overcome and reach full maturity in Christ. Suffering during persecution has far-reaching effects on the souls of others.

'We believe that the Lord gathers our tears and will pour them out upon the thirsty, seeking hearts of the Russian people,' said the Evangelical Christian Baptists of Russia in the above-cited letter of the second congress of their church council. Suffering and tears have power. During persecution many tears will be shed, not only because of the torment we must undergo ourselves. If we profess Jesus in such times, others are usually involved or – what is often harder to bear than our own suffering – we see our nearest and dearest made to suffer as well. All this means deep grief and heartache. But on the other hand we may find our suffering in persecution increased by those who are closest to us, because they are members of a Communist or an atheist organization – and that indeed causes us bitter anguish.

But how encouraging it is to know that 'the Lord gathers our tears and will pour them out'. Our tears will bring blessing to thirsty, seeking hearts. The grain of wheat falls into the ground during persecution, giving rise to new life at other places. Individuals and even whole groups of people receive new spiritual life, as is the case in Russia where revival has broken out in various districts. The martyrs are, and always will be, the seeds of the Church.

It is truly amazing that we are to be taken into the 'fellowship of his sufferings' (Phil. 3:10 AV), which means suffering with Jesus for the sake of His Church, for His elect, for those who seek God and for those who have fallen away from Him or live in direct rebellion against Him. The tears we shed during persecution, the agonizing suffering we undergo will help bring many to Jesus so that they can reach eternal glory. Suffering for Jesus, the King of kings, has far-reaching results.

The deeper and greater the suffering is, the more wonderful the fruit and glory will be. Accordingly, the agony endured during persecution in the cross-examinations and torture, which can often be so gruesome, will bear immeasurable fruit. If Jesus rewards us for giving a cup of cold water, then how much more will He reward those who undergo torture for His sake? Because He loves us so much, He shares our suffering, looking upon us in deep gratitude for all that we endure for His sake. Uplifted by this hope, the apostles, who encountered great hardships and had to go through the depths of suffering, were always joyful, but especially when they spoke of suffering. 'Rejoice in so far as you share Christ's sufferings, that you may also rejoice and be glad when his glory is revealed' (1 Pet. 4:13). It is eternity that counts. No words can express what awaits us in heaven, if we have suffered for Jesus in this life. There we shall behold His countenance and overwhelming joy will fill our hearts. Supreme delight awaits us for all eternity – jubilation, exultation and joyful laughter as compensation for all the tears we have shed here.

Heaven is a reality and it awaits our homecoming. The suffering of this lifetime will come to an end, but there is no end to the glory that is prepared for us above. If we live with our heart and soul in heaven where Christ is, we shall be able to bear the suffering during persecution. Hope and expectation of the future joy give us the strength to endure, and the crown of glory that is laid up for us makes all suffering worthwhile.

In Revelation 20, verse 4, the martyrs are promised that they will reign with Jesus, enthroned beside Him. What an amazing prospect! For all eternity to abide with Jesus, our first and foremost Love, our Bridegroom and King! In the face of such glory, suffering must fade away. 'I consider that the sufferings of this present time are not worth comparing with the glory that is to be revealed to us' (Rom. 8:18). These words of Scripture hold true for all suffering, but especially for the suffering in persecution.

The glory of heaven will bring us incomprehensible joy and bliss for all eternity, whereas the suffering of this life only lasts a limited amount of time. It passes by. It has an end. And later it will be banished from us for ever. If we are patient and steadfast in faith, suffering will bring us endless rejoicing, as Jesus promised, 'Blessed are you that weep now, for you shall laugh' (Luke 6:21). In heaven we shall rejoice at His side for ever and ever.

Heaven brings light in darkness. Heaven is stronger than hell, overcoming torture and transforming the diabolical conditions of prison camps. Let us live now

73

in the reality of the world above and all that awaits us there, and even when we are in the depths of suffering, persecution and torment, we shall not lose this source of everlasting joy.

Prayer

Lord Jesus,

You are with me, helping me, strengthening me.

In the midst of my suffering I immerse myself in Your suffering, submerging my will in Yours, which is pure goodness. And in all my fear and agony I take refuge in Your wounds.

As I turn my eyes upon You, Lord Jesus, I am comforted.

O Man of Sorrows, my heart clings to You.

All horror is banished, for You are with me, bringing healing to my soul and making me strong.

You are my Shield, and Your angels watch over me. And I know the Father will carry me through all suffering.

I will remain steadfast, for Your blood is my strength; it makes the weak strong.

Heaven is beckoning and the crown shines brightly. Soon my suffering will be over, and transformed into glory. So let me suffer with You and for You in the fellowship of love.

Amen

Preparation starts today!

1.   Every time difficulties and impossible situations arise now, I will believe in the omnipotence of God and His fatherly aid. I will not give place to worry, but completely trust in the Father's tender, loving care, for He never gives me more than I can bear and always has ways and means to help. Then by the time persecution breaks out, I shall be 'practised in faith' so that I can experience His aid.

2.   Now I will bear my small bodily ailments – pain, weakness and fatigue – in faith in the power of Jesus' blood that sustains me and renews my strength. Then I shall have practice for the future when the physical suffering will be far greater.

3.   Every time I am faced with hardship and meaninglessness, I will surrender my will, and when I am chastened, I will humble myself even more beneath the mighty hand of God. I will say, 'Yes, Father, Your judgments are just – and so are the ones to come.'

4.   I will look to Jesus ever anew, turning to Him with all my heart. And as I behold the Man of Sorrows, who is full of grief and affliction, the desire to suffer is implanted in my soul. I will look to Him, the mighty Victor, who has vanquished Satan and sin.

5.   In faith I will claim Jesus' redemption in my daily battle against my spirit of criticism, pride, stinginess,

envy, self-will, egoism, anger, the desires of the flesh, and bondage to people and things. Then sin will not be able to weaken me in the future, and if I should be taken to a concentration camp, I can be a witness for Jesus when living together with others, by radiating His love and peace.

6. I will bear every hardship, great or small, out of love for Jesus, so that when I have to undergo pain and torment in persecution, my natural reaction will be, 'I will bear it for Your sake, Jesus.'

7. I will live in close fellowship with Jesus now, conversing with Him at all times and doing everything for Him in love, so that love, which is the strongest power of all, will give me the strength to bear the suffering in the time of persecution.

8. I will lead a life of prayer now, so that I shall be able to pray later. Prayer will be my deliverance in times of loneliness, temptation, suffering and torment, and when I am forsaken. Prayer will bring me Jesus and heaven on earth.

9. Now I will fight resolutely against my fear of others and my desire to win their favour, love, respect and approval, so that I can overcome cowardice. I commit myself to making an uncompromising stand for the Lord. I want to seek only God's approval in all matters now so that later during persecution, I shall be willing to pay the price.

10. I will do good now to those who hurt me and treat me unjustly by blessing them and showing them love in thought, word and deed. Then later I shall be able to meet my persecutors the right way, not judging them, but humbled because of my own sin and meek like a lamb, full of mercy towards them.

11. Every time I am at a loss as to what to say in some situation or conversation, I will trust the Holy Spirit implicitly to guide me and give me His words, now and also at future trials and cross-examinations.

12. Today I will count on the reality of heaven, which Jesus brings into our lives, and abide in this hope, so that during persecution I can rejoice, saying, 'Suffering will come to an end, and everlasting glory will follow.'

Notes

1. Kenneth Goff, *Brain-washing – A Synthesis of the Russian Textbook on Psychopolitics* (Englewood, Colorado, USA, n.d.), p.3. Kenneth Goff was a fee-paying member of the Communist Party and voluntarily appeared before the Un-American Activities Committee in Washington, D.C. in 1939. His testimony can be found in Volume 9 of that year's Congressional Report.

2. Ibid., p.6.

3. E. Smit, *De gevaren van sensitivity training* (Stichting Moria, Amsterdam, 1972).

4. Goff, op. cit., pp.24, 30–32, 39, 54f., 61.

5. Ibid., p.44.

6. Ibid., pp.59f.

7. *Cura Brochero*, no. 9 (January 1973), reporting on J. A. Vrosky, *Manual de Infiltracion Religiosa* (Montevideo, Uruguay, 1971).

8. Fides (Rome, 1958).

9. *Non-Military Warfare in Britain* (Foreign Affairs Publ. Co., Ltd., 1966), pp.5f., quoting *Cinema Documents*, The Italian Communist Party, Issue No. 12, pp.224f.

10. George S. Schuyler, 'The Fall, From Decency To Degradation', *American Opinion* (Belmont, Massachusetts, January 1969), p.6.

11. M. Basilea Schlink, *Never Before in the History of the Church* (Bethany Fellowship, Inc., Minneapolis, Minnesota, USA, 1970 and Marshall, Morgan & Scott, London, 1972).

12. *The New York Times* (November 29, 1967), pp.6f.

13. Ibid., p.5.

14. *Prepare for Revolution*, Poster No. 1 (Militant Trade Union Committee, England).

15. *Socialist Revolution, Not Capitalist Reforms*, Poster No. 2 (Militant Trade Union Committee, England).

16. Prof. Dimitri Manuilsky, Chairman of the Executive Committee of the Comintern, in a lecture held at a military school of the Red Army. cf. Dieter Friede, *Das russische Perpetuum Mobile* (H. O. Holzner-Verlag, Würzburg, 1959), p.205.

17. J. Edgar Hoover, 'A Morality For Violence', *Christianity Today* (Washington, D.C., April 28, 1972), p.9.

18. *Die Welt* (Hamburg, August 10, 1973).

19. *Mitteilungen der Abadia Benedictina de San José del Avila* (Caracas, Venezuela, June 1973), p.2.

20. Karl Marx and Friedrich Engels, *Hist. Kritische Gesamtausgabe* (1927), vol. I, 1, 1, pp.9f.

21. D. G. Stewart-Smith, *The Defeat of Communism* (Ludgate Press, London, 1964), pp.222f.

22. Goff, op. cit., p.37, see also pp.29-40.

23. David Emerson Gumaer, 'Satanism – A Practical Guide to Witch Hunting', *American Opinion* (Belmont, Massachusetts, September 1970), pp.14f.

24. Arthur Lyons, *The Second Coming: Satanism in America* (Dodd, Mead & Co., New York, 1970).

25. David F. Webber, *Satan's Kingdom and the Second Coming* (The Southwest Radio Church of the Air, Oklahoma City, Oklahoma, USA, n.d.), p.2.

26. George S. Schuyler, op. cit., p.6.

27. 'Evil, Anyone?', *Newsweek*, vol. 78 (New York, August 16, 1971), p.56.

28. David Emerson Gumaer, op. cit., p.21f. This article contains an account of a personal interview with Anton LaVey.

29. 'Evil, Anyone?', p.56.

30. David F. Webber, op. cit., p.2.

31. 'Evil, Anyone?', p.56.

32. Ibid., p.56.

33. David Emerson Gumaer, op. cit., pp.2f.

34. 'The Occult: A Substitute Faith', *Time Magazine* (New York, June 19, 1972).

35. *Mitteilungen der Abadia Benedictina de San José del Avila*, p.5.

36. *Evangelische Kommentare* (October 1972), p.593.

37. Donald McGavran, 'Yes, Uppsala Betrayed the Two Billion: Now What?', *Christianity Today* (Washington, D.C., June 23, 1972), pp.16–18.

38. John C. Bennett, *Foreign Policy in Christian Perspective* (1966), p.94.

39. AP, *The News and Observer* (Raleigh, North Carolina, July 17, 1966).

40. Bishop Rudolf Graber, *Athanasius und die Kirche unserer Zeit* (Verlag Josef Kral, Abensberg, 1973), pp.69f., 73.

41. *Dein Reich komme, Mitteilungen vom Missionsbund Licht im Osten* (February 1972), p.8f.

42. *Neukirchener Kalender* (Kalenderverlag des Erziehungsvereins, Neukirchen-Vluyn, Germany.

43. *Christus dem Osten* (Frankfurt a.M., January 1973), p.7, cf. *Open Doors with Brother Andrew*, (Orange, California), vol. 2, no. 1, February/March 1973.

44. *Wegweisungen unseres Gründers, Vorträge von Pater Josef Kentenich* (Schönstatt – Familienwerk, Vallendar/Rhein, Germany, July 16, 1967), pp.30f.

45. Winrich Scheffbuch, *Christen unter Hammer und Sichel* (R. Brockhaus-Verlag, Wuppertal, Germany, 1972), p.101.

46. Ibid., p.44.

47. Ibid., p.46.

48. Father Titus Brandsma. Excerpts from a poem he wrote in the Gestapo prison in Scheveningen,Holland. He was later deported to the concentration camp in Dachau where he died.

49. *Der Christusbote* (Remscheid, Germany, newsletter of March/April 1973).

50. M. Basilea Schlink, *Well-spring of Joy, Songs of the Sisters of Mary for singing and praying* (Evangelical Sisterhood of Mary in England, 1971), no. 257.

Other books consulted for 'Satanism – Religion or Politics?'
Lindsey, Hal with C. C. Carlson, *Satan is Alive and Well on Planet Earth* (Oliphants and Lakeland Paperbacks, London, 1973).
White, John Wesley, Ph.D., *Re-entry* (Zondervan Publishing House, Grand Rapids, Michigan, USA, 1970).

Other books by M. Basilea Schlink for your further interest

COUNTDOWN TO WORLD DISASTER – Hope and Protection for the Future   96 pp.

Dark clouds hang menacingly over the nations and all mankind, and the world barometer indicates a violent storm. Many are questioning the reason for continuing to live since life seems futile and meaningless. This book is intended to help overcome such resignation. But that is not all! . . . Not only are we shown how to overcome fear, but we are offered the deepest fulfilment for our lives now in this chaotic age, and our eyes are set on the eternal hope.
(translated into Chinese, Danish, Dutch, Finnish, French, Indonesian, Italian, Norwegian, Swedish and Tagalog)

POLLUTION: but there *is* an Answer   64pp.

Only a decade ago, scientists were promising us a golden future for the world. Yet already they are pronouncing its death sentence. What has gone wrong? (translated into Dutch, Finnish, Italian, Norwegian and Swedish)

FOR JERUSALEM'S SAKE I WILL NOT REST 126pp.

Here the love of God for Israel is portrayed, and a

spotlight is cast upon the events of our times, giving
us a glimpse of God's ultimate plan.
(translated into Hebrew)

BEHOLD HIS LOVE   144pp.

Nothing can bring us closer to Jesus than meditating
upon His Passion, for in doing so we search the
depths of His heart. This book will help us to find a
warm, vital relationship with our Saviour when we
behold His amazing love which compelled Him to
choose suffering and death for our sakes.

FATHER OF COMFORT (Daily readings)   128pp.

God so often seems to be far away and in times of
sadness and misery it is difficult to realize that He
wants to reveal His fatherly love to us . . . These
readings help us to develop that close contact, a
personal relationship of love and childlike trust in the
Father, which we need in order to nurture our faith in
Him.
(translated into Arabic, Chinese, French, Greek,
Indonesian, Italian, Norwegian and Swedish)

MY ALL FOR HIM   162pp.

This book will warm the hearts of those who long to
love our dear Lord more. It will show them how to
experience the love of the Bridegroom . . . As the forces
of darkness move forward, nothing but the sufficiency
of the love of Christ filling our hearts will be great

enough to triumph against them. We need to be shown the way while there is time.
(translated into Greek, Indonesian, Italian and Norwegian)

YOU WILL NEVER BE THE SAME   192pp.

How can we overcome sin? Asked this question, M. Basilea Schlink set about prescribing 'spiritual medicine', dealing one by one with the sinful traits which mar the Christian's life, helping us to recognize them in ourselves and pointing out the remedy. (translated into Finnish, Italian, Norwegian and Swedish)